TIKTOK FOR BOOMERS

Join the latest viral craze!

Steve Quinn

CONTENTS

CHAPTER 1 - UNDERSTANDING TIKTOK AS A BOOMER

Welcome to TikTok for Boomers! In this book, we will explore the world of TikTok and how it can be used by those who may not have grown up with social media. If you're a Baby Boomer or older and have been hesitant to join the platform, this book is for you.

TikTok has quickly become one of the most popular social media apps in the world, with more than 1 billion active users. While many assume it is only for young people, there are actually a growing number of older users on the app, sharing funny videos, dancing along to popular songs, and even showcasing their talents.

In this book, we will provide a step-by-step guide on how to use TikTok from setting up your account to creating your first video. We will also cover some basic etiquette and safety tips that are important for all users to know.

But beyond just the technical aspects of TikTok, we will also explore why this app has become so popular and what it offers its users. From finding new hobbies to connecting with friends and family, TikTok can be a fun and engaging way to spend time online.

So whether you're looking to expand your online presence or simply want to understand what all the fuss is about, let's dive into TikTok for Boomers together!

TikTok is a social media platform that has become incredibly popular in the past few years. It started as an app called Musical.ly and was mainly used by young people to create short music videos. However, with the addition of new features and a change in its name, TikTok has expanded to include all kinds of content and users from all over the world.

As a Boomer, you might be wondering how this platform could possibly be relevant to you. After all, it's often associated with Generation Z and Millennials. But don't write it off just yet – there's plenty of fun to be had on TikTok no matter what your age is.

Let's start by taking a look at how the app works. When you first open TikTok, you'll see a feed of short videos created by other users. You can scroll through these videos by swiping up or down on your screen. If you find a video that you like, tap on it to watch it in full-screen mode.

As you continue using the app, TikTok's algorithm will learn what kind of content you enjoy watching and will start showing you more videos that align with your interests. This means that every user has a unique "For You" page where they can discover new creators and trends.

Speaking of trends – one of the things that makes TikTok so engaging is its constantly-evolving library of challenges and memes. These are usually centered around specific songs or ideas and often involve some kind of dance or lip sync element.

But not every video on TikTok needs to be part of a trend or challenge – there's plenty of room for creativity and self-expression too. Many users use the app as a way to share their thoughts or showcase their talents through comedy sketches, fashion tutorials, cooking demos, and more.

So why should Boomers give TikTok a try? For one, it's a great way to stay up to date with what younger generations are interested in. You might even find that you end up enjoying some of the content that they create! Additionally, using TikTok can be a fun and low-pressure way to explore your own creative side. If you've been looking for a new hobby to try out, making videos on the app could be just the thing.

Of course, there are also plenty of misconceptions about TikTok that need to be addressed. Some people assume that it's only for kids or that all of the content on the app is inappropriate. While it's true that there is some content on TikTok that might not be suitable for all ages, there are also plenty of ways to curate your feed so that you're only seeing things that you're comfortable with.

Another common misconception is that older generations aren't welcome on social media platforms like TikTok. While it's true that these apps are often associated with younger users, there's no reason why Boomers can't participate too. In fact, many older creators have found success on TikTok by sharing their experiences and wisdom with younger audiences.

So if you're still unsure about whether or not TikTok is right for you as a Boomer, I encourage you to give it a chance! Spend some time scrolling through your "For You" page and see if anything catches your eye. And who knows – maybe you'll end up becoming the next big thing on the platform!

CHAPTER 2 - CREATING A TIKTOK ACCOUNT

Welcome to Chapter 2, where we'll guide you through the process of creating your very own TikTok account. Follow these easy steps, and you'll be a part of the TikTok community in no time.

1. Download the app

The first step is to download TikTok from either the App Store or Google Play, depending on whether you have an iPhone or Android device.

2. Sign up with your email, phone number, or social media accounts

Once downloaded, head to the 'Sign Up' button on the bottom right corner of the screen. From there, you can choose whether to sign up with your email address, phone number or by linking your Facebook, Instagram or Twitter account.

3. Choose a username

Your username will be how other TikTok users identify you on the platform. Make sure it's unique and easy to remember. If possible, try and use one that is similar to usernames you use on other social media platforms.

4. Choose a profile picture

Your profile picture is another way for people to identify you on TikTok so select a photo that reflects who you are.

5. Write your bio

Your bio is where you can share some basic information about yourself so that viewers can get an idea about who they're following. Keep in mind that your bio needs to be short as it has a character limit of only 80 characters.

6. Explore TikTok's features

Now that you've created an account and set up your profile go ahead and explore some of what Tiktok has to offer.

- The 'Following' tab will show all videos posted by users who follow

- The 'For You' page will suggest videos based on what's popular or trending - this is also known as algorithmic feed

- The 'Discover' tab allows users to search for specific topics

Now let's get started with setting up your profile.

7. Editing your profile

You can edit your profile at any time by clicking on the icon on the bottom right corner of the screen and selecting 'Edit Profile'. Here you can change your profile picture, username, bio and even link to other social media profiles.

8. Navigating through Tiktok's functions

The home page or "Recommendations Page" is where most users explore content. The default autoplay setting will take users to another video once a video has finished playing. Users can swipe up or tap an arrow to browse content.

9. Finding friends on TikTok

To find friends on TikTok, click on the 'Discover' tab and type in their name in the search box. You can also connect with friends by linking your contacts list.

10. Creating a safe password

As with all apps, it's important that you create a strong password that ensures maximum account security.

- Use a combination of upper- and lower-case letters, numbers, and special characters.

- Avoid using common passwords such as '1234', 'password', or 'qwerty'

- Avoid using personal information such as your name or date of birth

In conclusion, creating an account on TikTok is easy, just follow these simple steps and make sure to customize your bio and select either an interesting photo or one that reflects who you are. Once you've created an account don't forget to explore some of the app's features like navigating through its different tabs (following/for you/discover), connecting with friends, customizing your profile via editing feature and creating secure passwords for maximum account security.

CHAPTER 3 - FOLLOWING TRENDING TOPICS

In this chapter, we will dive into the importance of following trending topics on TikTok. The platform is known for its viral challenges and trends that can reach millions of users in a matter of hours. By staying up to date with what's trending, you can effectively engage with the TikTok community and grow your audience.

Identifying current trends on TikTok through hashtags and challenges

Hashtags are a crucial element of TikTok, just like other social media platforms such as Instagram and Twitter. They help you identify posts related to a specific topic or challenge. For instance, if you want to know about dance-related content, search for #dancechallenge.

Challenges are also an excellent source to identify what's currently trending on the platform. Challenges range from simple lip-syncing videos to complex dance routines that require a lot of work. Some popular examples include the "Renegade Challenge" and the "Blinding Lights Challenge".

Staying up to date with trending topics by following key

influencers

Following key influencers can be an effective way to stay up to date with current trends on TikTok. Influencers typically have a large following and often participate in trending challenges before they gain mainstream attention.

Moreover, influencers can provide insights into user engagement patterns and help you understand why certain challenges go viral while others don't succeed as much.

Examples of recent popular challenges

One popular trend that took everyone by storm was the "Savage Challenge." This challenge involved dancing to Megan Thee Stallion's hit song "Savage" while performing hand gestures at specific points in the song.

Another example is the "Say So Dance Challenge," which featured Doja Cat's chart-topping hit song "Say So." The challenge involved performing a choreographed dance routine that mirrored Doja Cat's moves in her music video.

Tips for participating in challenges without compromising safety or privacy

While participating in challenges can be fun, it's crucial to take necessary precautions to ensure you don't compromise your privacy or safety.

Firstly, be mindful of the information you share on the platform. Avoid sharing personal information such as your phone number or address.

Secondly, if a challenge involves revealing your location, consider either not participating or using a fake location. Additionally, avoid posting videos that reveal sensitive information about yourself or others.

Finally, never feel pressured into engaging in a particular type of content if it makes you uncomfortable. Always remember that your privacy and safety come first.

Understanding why certain challenges go viral

TikTok is a platform where anything can go viral overnight. However, some challenges gain more traction than others. There are several factors behind this:

> ➤ Simplicity: Challenges that are easy-to-do and don't require much effort tend to be more popular among users.

> ➤ Memorable: Challenges that are unique and leave an impression on viewers are more likely to be shared or recommended to others.

> ➤ Universal appeal: Challenges that have universal appeal often get shared because they resonate with multiple communities and cultures.

> ➤ Entertainment value: Challenges that are entertaining and bring people together often have high engagement rates.

In conclusion, staying up to date with current trends by following hashtags, influencers and participating in trending challenges will help give you greater insight into what makes TikTok so popular. Just remember always to prioritize your safety before engaging in any type of content on the platform.

CHAPTER 4 – NAVIGATING THROUGH DIFFERENT CONTENT GENRES

In this chapter, we will discuss the various types of content genres that you can find on TikTok. TikTok is a platform that offers a diverse range of content for everyone, no matter your interests or age. From dance and lip-syncs to comedy and beauty, there is something for every person on this app.

Firstly, let's discuss the popular genre of dance videos. These videos feature users creating dances to popular songs, and they often go viral. Many people participate in these challenges, making it a fun way to engage with others around the world. Some dancers even teach others how to do the choreography in their videos.

A great example of this genre is @addisonre. Addison Rae is one of the most popular creators on TikTok and has made a name for herself by creating incredible dances. Her videos receive millions of views within a few hours, which makes her incredibly sought after by well-known brands and celebrities.

Another genre that users enjoy watching is lip-syncing. In these videos, users mouth the words to their favourite songs or sound bites from movies and TV shows. The trend started with musicals like Hamilton but has since taken off across all genres.

One creator who does an excellent job in carrying out lip-syncing challenges is @bellapoarch. She creates funny lip syncs using unique sounds that make her profile stand out from other creators.

Comedy is another popular genre on TikTok; creators make short skits or jokes that often have relatable humour that resonates with viewers globally. A trending comedian worth checking out is @trevornoah; he creates quick clips that are similar in style to his stand-up comedy routines.

Beauty influencers have also found success in utilizing Tik Tok solely as a platform to showcase their makeup skills and beauty tips with short-form visuals as opposed to traditional YouTube tutorials.

@jamescharles is an excellent example of a TikTok content creator who has successfully leveraged the platform to grow his beauty brand. He creates fresh looks and shares his favourite makeup products, making him a popular industry figure to follow.

Fashion is another genre that users enjoy on TikTok, and this platform has become a great way for influencers to showcase their style tips and techniques. The content ranges from DIY outfits videos to styling hacks that viewers can try out.

One of the best accounts for fashion inspiration is @zoelaz. She creates short-form video content showcasing her style expertise in creating killer outfits, often sharing where to purchase clothing items and accessories.

Now that you know about the various types of genres on TikTok let's talk about how you can find accounts aligned with your interests. You can search using hashtags related to your hobbies or favourite travel destinations, which will lead you towards creators who share similar interests as you.

If you're interested in gardening, for example, searching through hashtags like #gardeningtips #indoorgardening will show related videos uploaded by other users. From there, it's easy to follow the creators whose content resonates most with your interests.

In conclusion, TikTok may initially seem overwhelming due to its vast range of diverse content genres; however, once you familiarize yourself with them, it becomes an incredible platform for entertainment and learning. Whether dance videos or travel vlogs are your thing, there's something creative for everyone on this app- so jump right in and start exploring!

CHAPTER 5 - FOSTERING CREATIVITY & POSTING ENGAGING CONTENT

TikTok is all about creativity, and the app provides an excellent platform for creators to express themselves in unique ways. However, with the abundance of content on TikTok, it can be challenging to stand out from the crowd. In this chapter, we will discuss how you can foster creativity and post engaging content that sets you apart from others.

Stay Creative

Creativity is a vital factor in any form of content creation. Whether it's a painting or a video, creative input makes all the difference. TikTok is no exception; hence it is essential to stay creative while making videos for the platform.

The first step towards fostering creativity is finding inspiration. Inspiration comes from various sources, including music, art, and other creators on TikTok. For instance, if you are into dancing or lip-syncing, following your favourite dancers' accounts can inspire you to come up with new ideas for your videos.

Another way to stay creative is by trying something new every day. When creating content for TikTok, don't be afraid to experiment with different formats or themes – you never know what might go viral!

Avoid Reposted Content

While reposting popular content may seem like an easy way out of creating original content ideas, it might not be beneficial in the long run. Instead of reposting someone else's idea, try coming up with something unique that reflects your personality.

Creating original content also helps establish your brand identity and attracts followers who appreciate your creativity. It's always better to take inspiration from existing trends or challenges and put your spin on them rather than copying them entirely.

Editing Tools

One of the best things about TikTok's video creation tools is that they are easy to use and intuitive even for beginners. The app has several editing features such as filters, music library and text overlays that allow users to add their own unique touches to their videos.

Filters can transform the look and feel of your video, making it stand out from other TikTok content. Experiment with different filters to discover what works best for you.

Music is also an integral part of TikTok, and choosing the right track can make or break a video. The app's music library offers a broad selection of songs that you can use to add interest to your content. You can even create your own sound bites by recording original audio content.

Another editing tool that many creators use is text overlays. These are captions that appear on-screen and can help convey your message or add context to the video.

Using Humour

One of the most effective ways to engage with audiences on TikTok is humour. Humour is an excellent way to humanize yourself and connect with viewers on a personal level. Adding a touch of humour, be it through witty comments, funny expressions or well-timed actions in videos, can help increase engagement with your content.

However, keep in mind that everyone has a different sense of humour, so what may be funny to some people might not be so amusing to others. Therefore, it's important to experiment with different styles and see what works best for you.

Learn from Other Users' Creativity

Lastly, learning from other users' creativity is one of the best ways to improve your own content creation skills. By engaging with other creators' videos and taking inspiration from their work, you can learn new techniques and strategies for creating engaging content.

TikTok's algorithm suggests trending videos based on your preferences; this feature helps you discover new creators you might not have found otherwise. Watching popular creators in your niche or industry could give you new ideas or help refine existing strategies.

Conclusion

Fostering creativity and posting engaging content are crucial elements in building an active following on TikTok. With millions of active users daily, it's easy for videos to get lost without proper attention to detail. By staying creative, avoiding reposted content, using editing tools and humour, and learning from other creators on the platform, you can create unique content that stands out.

Remember, your followers want to see your personality through your content; so stay true to yourself and have fun while creating TikTok videos!

CHAPTER 6 - BUILDING YOUR FOLLOWING

So you've made the leap into the wonderful world of TikTok, and now it's time to start building your following. This can feel overwhelming at first, but with a few strategies and best practices, you'll be on your way to gaining views, followers, and maybe even going viral.

Building a Niche Based on Interests and Hobbies

One of the most important things you can do when building your following on TikTok is to find your niche. A niche is simply an area of interest or topic that you specialize in or are passionate about. Finding your niche will help you create content that is unique and engaging, which will attract more views and followers.

To find your niche, start by thinking about what topics or hobbies you enjoy talking about or sharing with others. For example, if you love cooking, consider creating cooking tutorials or sharing recipes. If you enjoy traveling, create videos showcasing your favourite destinations or providing tips for other travellers.

When creating content within your niche, it's important to be authentic and true to yourself. Don't try to copy other users' styles or content; instead, focus on what makes you unique and interesting. This will help build trust with your audience and keep them engaged over time.

Strategies for Getting More Views And Followers

Once you've found your niche and started creating content that's unique to you, it's time to start thinking about how to get more views and followers.

Firstly ensure that all platforms are interconnected, this includes Instagram/Facebook/Twitter as these social media channels can link back to each other.

One way of doing this is by consistently creating high-quality videos that are both entertaining and informative. This means paying attention not just to the visuals but also the sound quality as well as editing the video - snappy cuts work best on TikTok though so bear this mind when editing! Use transitions between takes which are consistent to make the video seem more fluid. Don't be afraid to experiment and see what content works best, it might take a few attempts but find the approach that worked well for previous videos and stick with it.

Another way of gaining followers is by engaging with other users. This means responding to comments on your videos as well as leaving comments on other users' videos. When you leave comments, try to add value by providing insights or asking questions, this helps build a community around your content.

It's also important to use hashtags effectively when uploading your videos to TikTok. Hashtags are used to categorize content and help users discover new videos based on their interests or hobbies. To find relevant hashtags for your niche, search for keywords related to your content and see what hashtags others are using in their posts.

Additionally, collaborate with other users within your niche can also help attract more followers. One way of collaborating is through "duets," which allow you to create a split-screen video with another user. Duets can be a great way of brainstorming ideas together or creating fun challenges and games for each other's audiences.

Best Practices for Responding to Comments/Engaging With Followers

One of the most important things you can do when building your following on TikTok is engage with your audience. This means responding to comments left on your videos as well as actively seeking out opportunities to connect with other users.

When responding to comments, always strive for professionalism and kindness - even if someone has left a negative comment or disagrees with something said in the video then being gracious will always work in one's favour.

Remember also that it's not just about replying but fostering connections between followers- group chats involving similar interests that share some common ground (e.g. cooking techniques) provide an opportunity not just between author and follower but followers themselves who may become fans each other's content - this builds loyalty amongst fans which is priceless when seeking the success of one's social media presence.

Effectively Using Hashtags to Increase Discoverability

As mentioned before, hashtags are vital to increase discoverability. Therefore, it's important to choose the right ones for your niche - use and research popular ones that relate to what you post. However, it's also important not to go overboard with hashtags as this may appear spammy and decrease engagement.

A general rule of thumb is between 3-5 hashtags per post, including one that you create yourself which others in your niche can also use.

Collaborating With Other Users Through "Duets" or Other Methods

Collaboration is a fantastic way of expanding one's reach on TikTok. It provides an opportunity to establish new connections and tap into other user's audiences.

Duets are a fantastic way of doing this- these can be done with anyone who has a public account simply by clicking the "share" option under their video and selecting "Duet". A shared piece of music or trend creates a unique experience where each creator adds their content side by side with each other.

In conclusion, building your following on TikTok requires finding your niche, creating high-quality content that is both entertaining and informative, engaging with your audience and collaborating with other users. But remember- above all else stay true to oneself!

CHAPTER 7 - NAVIGATING THROUGH PRIVACY SETTINGS

In this Chapter, we'll be discussing the importance of managing your privacy settings on TikTok. As you may already know, TikTok is a social media app that allows users to create and share short videos with others. While it can be a fun and exciting platform to use, it's important to take your privacy seriously.

First and foremost, it's essential to understand the app's data collection policies. TikTok collects information from its users such as location data, device information, and usage data. This information is then used for targeted advertising and algorithmic recommendations. However, if you're not comfortable with this data collection or are concerned about your privacy, there are steps you can take to limit how much information is shared.

To manage your privacy settings on TikTok, start by going into your account settings. From there, click on "Privacy" and you'll be presented with several options for controlling who can see your content and personal information. For example, you can choose whether or not you want others to be able to see your likes or comments.

Another important aspect of privacy is controlling the visibility of personal information such as your location or phone number.

By default, these pieces of information are private but can be shared if you choose to add them onto your profile. If you're worried about people finding out too much about you or using this information inappropriately, it's best to keep these details hidden.

As you start promoting your account on TikTok, it's also important to stay safe online. One way to do this is by being aware of who has access to your videos and what they may do with them. Make sure that only people who follow you or are approved followers have access to view them.

Additionally, reporting cyber-bullying and inappropriate content should never be taken lightly on any social media platform - including Tiktok. If someone is being mean or harassing you in the comments section, it's important to report the user and their account. Tiktok has a feature where you can report an account for violating community guidelines, and they will take appropriate action that may include removing content or banning users.

Overall, managing your privacy settings on TikTok is crucial to maintaining your safety while still enjoying the benefits of using the app. Don't be afraid to take advantage of these settings and make changes as needed. Remember, your privacy is important and worth protecting!

CHAPTER 8 - CREATING VIRAL CONTENT

By now, you understand the basics of TikTok and how to create engaging content. But what if you want to take your TikTok game to the next level? What if you want your videos to go viral, reaching millions of people all over the world? In this chapter, we will be discussing tips on creating content that goes viral on TikTok.

Analyzing the Algorithm

Before we dive into creating viral content, it is essential to understand how the algorithm works. The algorithm is responsible for showing users their "For You" page, which is where most viral videos are found. When a user opens TikTok, they are brought straight to their "For You" page instead of their followers' content.

TikTok's algorithm works by analyzing a user's behaviour and engagement patterns. If a user likes or comments on a particular type of video, TikTok will show them more similar videos. Therefore, if you want your video to go viral, it needs to catch the attention of viewers and keep them engaged enough for TikTok's algorithm to recognize it as popular.

Timing Posts for Optimal Engagement

When posting on TikTok, timing is crucial. You must publish content at a time when your target audience is most active online. If your audience consists primarily of Boomers who work nine-to-five jobs or retirees who follow strict schedules during the day, then morning or evening hours may be ideal.

Another crucial aspect to consider is posting frequency. Posting consistently builds trust with followers and lets them know when they can expect new content from you; hence they can be more likely to engage with your posts.

Strategies for Using Tags and Keywords Effectively

TikTok has an extensive library of music tracks and sound effects that creators can use in their videos. Utilizing popular music tracks and trending sounds can help increase the visibility of your videos. Additionally, using relevant hashtags and keywords can make your content more discoverable.

When choosing hashtags, ensure they are relevant to your video's content and audience. Popular and trending hashtags are also beneficial. You can see which hashtags are popular on TikTok by checking out the "Discover" page or doing a quick search in the app's search bar.

Examples of Successful Viral Videos on TikTok

Perhaps one of the best ways to create viral content is by analyzing successful videos from other creators. Here are some examples of what has worked for others:

- ➢ Dance Challenges: Many of the most viral videos on TikTok involve dance challenges where users create their unique choreography to a song or sound bite.

- ➢ Pet Videos: Cute animal videos never go out of style, so why not showcase your furry friends' skills and talents?

➢ Lip-Syncing: While lip-syncing may seem outdated, it is still prevalent on TikTok with many creators putting their spin on famous movie scenes or songs.

➢ Educational Content: Despite being known for short-form entertainment, educational content on topics such as science or history has been successful among younger audiences.

➢ DIY Projects: DIY tutorials showcasing simple recipes, home decor ideas, or craft projects have become increasingly popular during lockdowns across the world.

➢ Comedy Sketches: Short comedy sketches that resonate with viewers can gain incredible traction on TikTok.

In Conclusion

Creating viral content requires a combination of strategy, timing, creativity and luck! However, understanding how TikTok's algorithm works can be incredibly helpful in increasing your chances of virality. Remember to experiment with different types of content while staying true to your brand identity and values as a Boomer creator.

Take time to analyze what type of content works best for you by keeping track of engagement metrics such as views, likes, comments and shares. Lastly, always have fun and be authentic in your creations; after all, TikTok is an app that celebrates creativity, humour and authenticity.

CHAPTER 9 - INFLUENCER MARKETING OPPORTUNITIES

In recent years, influencer marketing has become a popular way for brands and businesses to reach their target audience. With the rise of social media platforms like TikTok, more and more influencers are emerging who have built strong followings and are able to leverage their influence to promote products or services.

So, what exactly is influencer marketing? In simple terms, it involves collaborating with individuals who have a large following on social media in order to promote your brand or product. Influencers can be anyone from celebrities to regular people who have built a following based on their niche content.

TikTok provides an incredible opportunity for brands and businesses to connect with their target audience through influencer marketing. The platform has over 1 billion active users worldwide, with the majority being under the age of 30. This demographic is highly coveted by advertisers as they are seen as early adopters of new trends and technologies.

One of the most important aspects of building a successful influencer marketing campaign on TikTok is having a strong following. When considering potential influencers to collaborate with, it's important to look at not only their follower count but also the engagement rate on their videos. An influencer may have a million followers, but if their engagement rate is low then they may not be an effective partner for your brand.

Finding potential sponsors or brands to work with can be done through outreach or by using influencer marketing platforms such as Upfluence or AspireIQ. These platforms allow brands to connect with influencers across various social media platforms including TikTok.

When it comes to sponsored content on TikTok, it's important that influencers disclose that the content is sponsored by using hashtags such as #ad or #sponsored. This ensures that viewers are aware that the content they are watching is promotional and not organic.

The Federal Trade Commission (FTC) requires influencers to clearly disclose any sponsorship relationships in their TikTok videos. Failure to do so can result in fines or legal action. It's important for influencers to understand the FTC disclosure requirements and ensure that their sponsored content complies with these guidelines.

One example of a successful branded content campaign on TikTok is the campaign launched by e.l.f. Cosmetics. The brand collaborated with several influencers on the platform to create makeup tutorials featuring their products. The videos went viral, resulting in millions of views and significant brand exposure.

Another example is the Chipotle Guac Dance Challenge, which was launched in partnership with influencer David Dobrik. The challenge involved users creating their own dance moves to a song about guacamole, with winners receiving free burritos for a year. The challenge quickly gained traction on TikTok and resulted in thousands of user-generated videos featuring Chipotle's products.

In conclusion, influencer marketing on TikTok provides an

incredible opportunity for brands and businesses to connect with their target audience through creative and engaging content. Building strong relationships with influencers who have a large following and high engagement rate is crucial, as is understanding FTC disclosure requirements for sponsored content. With the right approach, influencer marketing can be an effective way to drive sales and increase brand awareness on TikTok.

CHAPTER 10 – USING TIKTOK FOR BUSINESS PURPOSES

In this chapter, we'll be discussing how you can leverage TikTok to promote your business, products or services. With over 1 billion active users, Tik Tok is a powerful platform that offers unique opportunities for businesses seeking to reach a younger and broader audience. Let's dive in!

Successfully promoting businesses, products or services on TikTok.

Tik Tok offers diverse opportunities for businesses to promote themselves effectively. To get started, create a company account on the app and start posting short-form videos that showcase your brand's personality and unique selling proposition. Remember that TikTok is all about creativity! So try to incorporate a bit of humour or use trending sounds and challenges relevant to your brand.

To successfully promote your business, you need to create content that resonates with your target audience. But who exactly is using Tik Tok? According to recent surveys, the majority of users are between the ages of 16-24 years old, with female users outnumbering males. However, there are also significant numbers of people outside this age range who use the app regularly.

When creating content for your target audience on Tiktok make sure it's entertaining as well as informative enough, so viewers know exactly what service or product you're providing. This can be achieved by leveraging humour and music popular among the viewer's demographic.

Another way to boost engagement on Tiktok is by collaborating with influencers or other brands within your industry. Influencers have an established following that trusts their opinion; partnering with them can help increase brand awareness and drive traffic towards your page.

Developing a social media strategy utilizing the most effective tools within the app

Once you've created your account and begun posting content regularly, it's essential to develop a social media strategy that aligns with your brand goals.

One effective way to do so is by using hashtags. Hashtags allow users looking for specific content related to your brand to find your videos easily. So, it is essential to optimize hashtags around the products and services you offer.

Another Tik Tok feature that can be used in your social media strategy is advertising. Tik Tok offers several advertising options that allow businesses to target specific demographics based on age, gender, location, interests etc. However, these ads do require some capital investment to ensure optimal performance.

Case studies showcasing business success stories on Tiktok

Several brands have leveraged TikTok's unique capabilities to create viral content and increase their brand awareness. For instance, Chipotle launched a challenge on the app with the hashtag #GuacDance. Users had to showcase their dance moves while holding avocados to win free guacamole from the restaurant chain. The challenge went viral with users posting more than 250k videos within six days of launch.

Another success story is American skincare brand E.L.F Cosmetics' "Eyes Lips Face" campaign. The company utilized influencers who created dance trends for the hashtag #eyeslipsface. Within a week of launching this campaign, there were over 3 million videos featuring the hashtag created by influencers and consumers alike.

Such case studies are crucial learning points for businesses looking at using TikTok as part of their marketing strategies.

Discussing how different industries can benefit from using Tiktok

The possibilities of how different industries can use Tik Tok are endless! Here are a few ideas:

> Fashion: Use TikTok to showcase new fashion lines or provide fashion tips.

> Travel: Showcase travel experiences or offer travel tips

> Food: Showcasing recipes or behind-the-scenes footage in restaurants.

> Fitness: Providing fitness tips or tutorials using popular music beats.

> Education: Use the platform to make educational content fun and exciting!

> Gaming Industry - Use live gameplay streaming for engagement and promotion.

In conclusion, TikTok offers an innovative approach for businesses looking to engage with a younger audience. The platform offers vast opportunities to create viral content, engage with influencers, and target specific demographics through ads. However, it's essential to develop a social media strategy that aligns with your brand goals and resonates with your target audience.

CHAPTER 11 - CELEBRATING DIVERSITY ON TIKTOK

TikTok has become a platform that celebrates diversity in all forms. The app is home to millions of users from different cultures, races, and backgrounds. It creates an environment where people can connect, share their stories, and celebrate their differences. In this chapter, we will explore the importance of diversity on TikTok and highlight some accounts created by people from diverse backgrounds. We will also emphasize inclusivity in creating new content ideas and address issues related to racism, sexism, and gender identity among other things in the TikTok community.

Firstly, it's important to understand that diversity is not just about race or ethnicity. It encompasses many aspects such as gender identity, sexual orientation, physical abilities, religion, socio-economic status and more. This is reflected in the TikTok user base which includes people from different backgrounds who have come together to create a vibrant community.

One example of an account that highlights diversity is @ddlovato. Demi Lovato has been very vocal about her struggles with mental health and addiction as well as being an advocate for LGBTQ+ rights. She uses her platform on TikTok to encourage self-love and acceptance while celebrating individuality.

Another account that showcases diverse voices is @tiktokwellness which features wellness tips from therapists who specialize in working with marginalized communities. They provide strategies for coping with stressors such as racism or discrimination while also promoting self-care practices like meditation or journaling.

@iamtabithabrown is another great example of how TikTok celebrates diversity. Tabitha Brown became famous on the platform for her vegan cooking tutorials which range from traditional African American dishes to more modern recipes using plant-based ingredients. Her goal is to inspire people to try new foods while embracing their cultural heritage.

These are just a few examples of the many accounts on TikTok that represent diverse voices. By following these creators, users can learn about experiences beyond their own while also gaining insights into other cultures.

In addition to highlighting diverse voices, it's important to emphasize inclusivity in creating new content ideas. This can be achieved by actively seeking out different perspectives and avoiding harmful stereotypes or assumptions.

One way to do this is by collaborating with people from different backgrounds. This not only helps bring a variety of experiences to the table but also promotes understanding and tolerance across different communities. For instance, a fashion influencer could collaborate with a designer from a marginalized community to showcase their designs and promote their brand.

Another way to create inclusive content is by using language that is respectful and non-offensive. Avoiding terms that are derogatory or stigmatizing can go a long way in making all users feel welcome on the platform.

However, despite the celebration of diversity on TikTok, issues related to racism, sexism and gender identity continue to plague the app. It's important for users to remain vigilant against these harmful behaviours and speak up when necessary.

Racism on TikTok takes many forms including hate speech, cyberbullying or excluding certain groups from participation in trends or challenges. Users should report any instances of racism they encounter on the platform, even if it means reporting someone they may know personally.

Sexism is also an issue on TikTok where women are often targeted with sexist comments or harassment. This can happen in response to videos that discuss feminist issues, body positivity or sexual orientation. Women should feel safe speaking up against misogyny and if necessary, reaching out for help if they feel threatened in any way.

The issue of gender identity on TikTok is complex as it involves both external attacks as well as internalized biases. Transgender users are often subjected to discrimination and abuse both online and offline which can have devastating consequences for their mental health. It's important for users to support trans individuals by amplifying their voices and pushing for more trans representation both among creators and viewership.

In conclusion, diversity is an essential aspect of TikTok and it's important to celebrate the different voices that make up the platform. By highlighting diverse creators, emphasizing inclusivity in content creation and remaining vigilant against issues related to racism, sexism, and gender identity, we can create a welcoming space for all users.

CHAPTER 12 - PROTECTING YOURSELF ON TIKTOK

In this chapter, we will be discussing the importance of protecting yourself on TikTok. As with any social media platform, it is important to ensure your safety and security when using TikTok.

Firstly, let's talk about strategies for protecting yourself online from potential threats. A good rule of thumb is to always keep your personal information private. This includes your full name, address, phone number and any other sensitive details that could be used to identify or locate you. Avoid sharing any personal information in your profile or comments section. Do not engage with strangers who may ask for personal information or try to start a conversation outside of the app.

Another key aspect of staying safe on TikTok is knowing how to handle cyberbullying and hate speech. Unfortunately, these issues are prevalent on all social media platforms and TikTok is no exception. If you receive negative comments or messages on your videos or profile, the best approach is to ignore them and report the user immediately. You can do this by selecting the three-dot icon next to their comment and selecting "Report". Remember that cyberbullying is never acceptable behaviour and it's important to stay strong in the face of negativity.

It's also important to be aware of fake accounts and false

information spread through the platform. There are many fake accounts on TikTok that impersonate celebrities, influencers or even friends in order to scam users out of money or gain access to personal information. Be cautious when engaging with accounts that seem suspicious or ask for payment for services such as shoutouts or promotions.

Additionally, there has been an increase in false information being spread across social media platforms including TikTok. This includes conspiracy theories, misinformation about current events and fake news stories designed to further agendas or spark controversy. Always fact-check any information before sharing it with others on TikTok.

Finally, let's discuss tips for staying safe in real life while engaging with strangers on TikTok. It's important to remember that not everyone on the internet is who they claim to be. Be cautious when interacting with strangers on TikTok and never give out personal information such as your address or phone number. If you decide to meet up with someone in real life that you met through TikTok, ensure that it is in a public place and let someone close to you know where you will be.

In conclusion, protecting yourself on TikTok is essential for a safe and enjoyable experience on the platform. Remember to keep your personal information private, handle cyberbullying and hate speech appropriately, be aware of fake accounts and false information, and stay safe when interacting with strangers in real life. By following these guidelines, you can enjoy using TikTok without compromising your safety or security.

CHAPTER 13 - STAYING RELEVANT ON TIKTOK

TikTok is the fastest-growing social media platform in the world right now, and it's not just for Gen Z anymore. More and more Boomers are joining the app every day to share their content, connect with others, and have some fun. But with such a rapidly evolving app, how can you stay relevant and keep up with the latest trends?

In this chapter, we'll explore why staying up to date with trends is crucial to remaining relevant on TikTok. We'll also discuss how to keep an eye on new features being added to the app, how to follow accounts of younger generations to stay informed about what's "cool," and how to continuously innovate with different types of content creation.

Why Staying Up to date With Trends is Crucial

TikTok is all about what's trending right now. Whether it's a new dance craze or a viral challenge, staying up to date with trends is crucial if you want your content to be seen by as many people as possible.

One way to stay up to date with trends is by following popular accounts on the app. This will give you an idea of what types of content are resonating with audiences at any given time. Another way is by checking out the "For You" page regularly. This page shows you content that TikTok thinks will be of interest to you based on your viewing habits.

And don't forget about hashtags! Hashtags are a great way to discover new content related to specific topics or trends. By using relevant hashtags in your own posts, you increase your chances of being discovered by others who are interested in those same topics.

Keeping an Eye on New Features Being Added

TikTok is constantly adding new features and tools for creators to use. From filters and effects to editing tools and sound libraries, there's always something new to try out.

It's important to keep an eye on these new features and incorporate them into your content when appropriate. For example, if TikTok introduces a new AR filter that fits with the theme of your video, try using it to make your content more engaging.

Another way to stay on top of new features is by following the official TikTok account on the app. This account shares updates about new features and provides tips for creators looking to improve their content.

Following Accounts of Younger Generations

As a Boomer on TikTok, it's important to recognize that you're sharing a space with younger generations. Following accounts of younger generations can give you insight into what's currently trending and what kind of content is popular among younger audiences.

Don't be afraid to engage with younger creators as well! Commenting on their posts or collaborating with them can help you both reach new audiences and learn from each other.

Continuous Innovation in Content Creation

The key to staying relevant on TikTok is continuous innovation in your content creation. This means not being afraid to try out new things and experiment with different types of content.

For example, if you usually create lip-sync videos, try branching out into other types of content like vlogs or tutorials. Or, if you typically use the same editing style for all of your videos, try switching it up by incorporating new effects or transitions.

Innovation can also come from collaborating with other creators or incorporating user-generated content into your own posts. By working together and sharing ideas, you can create unique and engaging content that stands out from the crowd.

Conclusion

Staying relevant on TikTok requires constant attention and effort. By staying up to date with trends, keeping an eye on new features being added to the app, following accounts of younger generations, and continuously innovating in your content creation, you'll be well-equipped to keep up and thrive in this rapidly growing social media platform.

So don't shy away from trying out new things and pushing yourself creatively. With some dedication and hard work, you'll be sure to make your mark on TikTok!

CHAPTER 14 - COLLABORATING WITH OTHER USERS

Collaboration is one of the best ways to grow your following on TikTok. It's also a great way to expand your creativity and connect with other like-minded people. In this chapter, we'll discuss the various collaborative opportunities available on TikTok, methods for finding potential collaborators, benefits of collaborating, and successful examples of collaboration-related challenges.

Overview of Collaborative Opportunities Available on Tik Tok

There are several collaborative opportunities that you can take advantage of on TikTok. Here are some of the most popular options:

> Duets: This is the most common type of collaboration on TikTok. A duet is when you create a video alongside another user's video. You can either add your own creative spin or react to their video in real-time.

> Challenges: Challenges are another great way to collaborate with other users. These challenges usually involve creating a video following specific rules or guidelines set by another user or group.

> Group Projects: Group projects require coordination between multiple users to create a final product. It can

be anything from lip-syncing together to creating a dance routine.

➢ Q&A Sessions: Q&A sessions require two users to go live and answer questions from their followers at the same time.

Best Methods for Finding Potential Collaborators

Finding potential collaborators may seem daunting at first, but there are many ways to find like-minded individuals who are interested in collaborating with you.

➢ Use Hashtags: Using hashtags related to your interests will make it easier for other users who share those interests to find you and potentially collaborate with you.

➢ Browse Explore Page: The explore page will show you content based on what you've liked and watched before which could lead you towards finding potential collaborators whose content relates more closely towards yours than other creators on the app.

➢ Engage With Other Users: Engaging with other users' content by liking, commenting, and sharing their videos can lead to a conversation that could lead towards collaboration.

➢ Collaborate With Others in Your Network: If you have friends or contacts who are also on TikTok, they may be interested in collaborating with you regularly.

Benefits of Collaborating

Collaborating with other users can provide many benefits, including:

➢ Increased Exposure: Collaborations help expose your content to new audiences and followers who might not have found your profile otherwise.

➢ More Engagement: Collaborations tend to receive higher engagement rates than individual videos because people are more likely to comment, like, and share when they see multiple people interacting in a video.

➢ Learning New Skills: Collaborating with other users can teach you new skills and techniques that you can apply to future videos.

Successful Examples of Collaboration-Related Challenges

Here are some successful examples of collaboration-related challenges on TikTok:

#FliptheSwitch Challenge - This challenge involved two users standing in front of a mirror while one person turns off the light switch and the other person switches clothes while dancing to Drake's song "Nonstop." The challenge went viral as celebrities joined in on the fun.

#BlindingLightsChallenge - This challenge was created by @gregdahl7 and involved couples creating a simple dance routine to The Weeknd's song "Blinding Lights." It became so popular that The Weeknd himself created a compilation video featuring some of the best entries.

#SaySoChallenge - This challenge was started by TikTok user @yodelinghaley using Doja Cat's song called "Say So". When Haley's video went viral, thousands of people replicated her choreography and created their own versions worldwide using the same sound clip.

Conclusion

Collaboration is an excellent way to grow your audience on TikTok while expanding your creative horizons. Use hashtags, browse explore page, engage with other users and collaborate with others in your network are all great methods to find potential collaborators. You can collaborate with other users using duets, challenges, group projects, or Q&A sessions. Collaborating opens up many benefits such as increased exposure, more engagement, and learning new skills which help you create better videos in the future. By following the successful examples of collaboration-related challenges, you can make your content viral and build a strong presence on TikTok.

CHAPTER 15 - LEARNING FROM YOUR ANALYTICS

Analytics can be a powerful tool to help you grow your account and gain popularity on TikTok. In this chapter, we will explore the different aspects of analytics and how you can use them to improve your TikTok presence.

Understanding Analytics through the App in Detail

Before we dive into understanding analytics, let's first understand what they are. Analytics are simply data that is collected about your account's performance on TikTok. This data can include information such as views, likes, shares, comments, and more.

To access your analytics on TikTok, go to your profile page and click on the three dots in the top right corner. From there, select "Analytics." Here you will find information about your account's performance over the last 7 or 28 days.

Exploring How Analytics Can Help You Grow Your Account

Now that we understand what analytics are let's explore how they can help us grow our accounts. One of the primary benefits of using analytics is that they provide insights into areas of our account that need improvement or attention.

For example, if you notice that a particular video has a high number of views but low engagement rate (likes/comments), then perhaps you need to improve the quality of your content or consider changing up your posting strategy. On the other hand, if engagement rates are high but views are low, then maybe you need to work on promoting your content more effectively.

Highlighting Key Performance Indicators (KPIs)

Key Performance Indicators (KPIs) are specific metrics used to measure an account's performance on TikTok. Some KPIs include views, likes, comments, shares, follower growth rate and engagement rate.

Engagement rate measures how much interaction a post receives from followers compared to its reach potential; it helps gauge audience interest in a particular post. It is calculated by taking the sum of likes, comments and shares on a post and dividing by the number of views.

Using Analytics to Refine Posting Strategy

Once you understand your account's performance using analytics, you can use that information to refine your posting strategy. This means focusing on the timing of posts, types/genre of videos etc.

Timing of Posts: When you notice the peak hours when most of your followers are active, focus on posting during those times. This will increase the likelihood that a larger audience sees your content when they're scrolling through their TikTok feed.

Types/Genre of Videos: Pay attention to the type or genre of videos that receive more engagement compared to others; focus on creating more content around that genre. This involves experimenting with different formats and themes until you find what clicks.

In conclusion, analytics can be an incredibly powerful tool for understanding how your TikTok account is performing. By utilizing KPIs such as views, likes, comments and engagement rate, we can gain insights into areas where our posts are performing well or need improvement. By refining our posting strategy based on these insights, we can improve our chances at gaining popularity on TikTok. So give it a try and see how analytics can help you grow your presence today!

CHAPTER 16 - FINDING A COMMUNITY WITHIN THE APP

In this chapter, we will discuss how to find a community within the app. TikTok is known for its vast and diverse community, and it's easy to get lost in the sea of content. Finding like-minded people with whom you can connect can help you feel more at home on the app and keep you engaged. Here are some ways to find your tribe on TikTok.

Connecting with Like-Minded Users Through Shared Interests and Hobbies

The easiest way to find a community on TikTok is through shared interests or hobbies. Whether it's cooking, gardening, singing, or gaming, there's a good chance that someone else on the app shares your passion. You can start by searching for hashtags related to your interests—for example, #gardeningtips or #singingcovers—and scrolling through the content that pops up. If you see a video that resonates with you, give it a like or leave a comment. This will show the user that you appreciate their content and may prompt them to check out your profile if they share similar interests.

You can also use the search function to look up specific topics or keywords related to your interest. When you find an account that posts about similar things as yours, don't hesitate to follow them and engage with their content.

Joining Groups or Communities Related To Specific Topics

Another way to find like-minded users is by joining groups or communities related specifically to your hobby/interests. Many creators form groups where they share tips on specific topics such as cooking, fashion or art tutorials. Joining these groups can give you access not only useful tips but also other creators who share common interests with you.

To join a group in TikTok, simply search for hashtags commonly used in these communities – such as #artcommunity or #fishinggroup – and browse through some of its videos. When joining, keep in mind that some groups may require permission, so be respectful of their rules.

Participating in Live Streams with Other Users

Another way to find and engage with like-minded users is through live streams. Many TikTok creators use this feature to connect directly with their followers and other creators, answering questions or just chatting about general topics. Some even organize challenges or games during the live stream to keep things fun.

To join a live stream, first look out for notifications about ongoing ones. You can also find them on your For You Page by searching for #livestreams on TikTok. Once you find an interesting one, click on it and send a request to join the livestream if possible. You'll want to make sure you have something valuable to add to the conversation before requesting a chat.

Engaging in Virtual Events Organized By Other Users

Lastly, engaging in virtual events organized by users can help connect you with others sharing similar interests while being fun at the same time. For example, someone interested in cooking may organize a virtual potluck where everyone prepares a dish and shares it on Tik Tok as they 'meet' online. Similarly, music lovers may hold virtual open mic nights where participants can showcase their talent.

These events are usually promoted through hashtags such as #virtualparties or #virtualmeetups so check those out often! Keep an eye out for cool contests too - some even offer prizes!

In conclusion

Finding a community within TikTok's vast userbase can be overwhelming but it's essential for staying engaged and connected on the app. Start by looking up hashtags related to your interests, follow Creators that post about similar topics as yours and engage with their content regularly. Joining groups, participating in Livestreams, and attending Virtual Events are all excellent avenues for finding like-minded people within the app's ecosystem.

We hope that these tips were helpful in connecting you with others who share your interests on TikTok. Remember, the app is all about fun and creativity, so don't hesitate to experiment and find what truly resonates with you!

CHAPTER 17 - ENJOYING TRENDING MUSIC & DANCES

In this chapter, we will be discussing the importance of enjoying trending music and dances on TikTok. TikTok is a platform that has become famous for its short-form videos featuring popular songs and dance moves. Therefore, it is essential to stay up to date with the latest trends in music and dancing to make the most out of your TikTok experience.

One of the best ways to enjoy trending music on TikTok is by listening to curated playlists featuring popular songs from different genres. These playlists are updated regularly, ensuring that you always have access to the latest hits. TikTok's algorithm also curate's playlists based on your listening preferences, making it easier for you to discover new songs that you might enjoy.

To find curated playlists on TikTok, simply head over to the 'Discover' tab located at the bottom of your screen. Here you will see various categories such as 'For You', 'Following', and 'Discover'. Under 'Discover', click on 'Sounds' and select any genre that interests you. This will take you to a page where you can browse through different songs within that category.

Apart from curated playlists, TikTok also features a variety of dance challenges set to popular songs. These challenges have become so popular that they often go viral and spread rapidly across social media platforms. Participating in these challenges can help increase your visibility on TikTok as well as connect you with other users interested in similar content.

There are numerous dance styles currently popular on TikTok, each with its unique moves, rhythm, and vibe. Let's take a closer look at some of these styles:

➤ The Renegade: This is one of the most popular dances on TikTok right now. It involves a series of arm movements coupled with legwork and footwork done in sync with K Camp's "Lottery (Renegade)" song.

➤ Say So: This dance is set to the Doja Cat song "Say So". It involves smooth and fluid movements that are relatively simple to learn, making it a popular option for beginners.

➤ Savage: This dance, created by TikTok user Keara Wilson, is set to Megan Thee Stallion's "Savage" song. It involves a series of arm and leg movements that require a bit of coordination.

➤ Blinding Lights: This dance is set to the song "Blinding Lights" by The Weeknd. It involves some fast-paced footwork and arm movements.

Participating in these trending dances can help increase your visibility on TikTok as well as keep you engaged with the latest trends on the app. Here are some tips for creating content featuring trending dances:

➤ Practice, practice, practice: Before recording your video, take some time to learn the moves thoroughly. You can slow down the videos or even break them down into different sections to make it easier for you to learn.

➤ Film in a well-lit area: Good lighting is essential when filming on TikTok. Make sure you're filming in a brightly lit area where your face and body are clearly visible.

➤ Use hashtags: Using relevant hashtags on your posts can help increase visibility and engagement. For example, if you're doing the Renegade challenge, use #renegadechallenge or #lotteryrenegade so that other users looking up these challenges can find your post easily.

Apart from participating in trending dances, you can also create original choreography inspired by current trends. Creating original content sets you apart from others and showcases your creativity. Here are some tips for creating original choreography:

➤ Listen to popular music across different genres: Keep an ear out for new songs across different genres such as pop, hip-hop, R&B, etc., and try creating choreography that complements the beat and rhythm of the song.

➤ Experiment with different moves: Don't be afraid to try new moves or steps that haven't been done before. This can help you create more unique and interesting content that sets you apart from other users.

➤ Engage with your audience: Once you've posted your original choreography, encourage your followers to engage with it by asking for feedback, suggestions, or even creating a challenge around it.

In conclusion, enjoying trending music and dances on TikTok is an essential part of the app experience. By participating in challenges and creating original content inspired by trends, you can increase your visibility and engagement on the app while staying up to date with the latest trends.

CHAPTER 18 - ENCOURAGING FAMILY & FRIENDS TO JOIN

Ah, the good old days of Facebook. It seems like just yesterday when we were all posting updates about our lives and seeing what our friends and family were up to. But now, there's a new player in town: TikTok. And while it may seem like it's just for the younger generation, there are actually many benefits to having your family and friends join you on this fun app.

First and foremost, TikTok is a great way to stay connected with loved ones who may live far away or who you may not get to see often. With the ability to create and share videos, you can keep everyone updated on what you're doing in a fun and engaging way. Plus, watching each other's videos can be a great way to share laughter and happy moments, even if you can't physically be together.

But let's be real - convincing your parents or grandparents to join TikTok may be easier said than done. So here are some tips for teaching them how to navigate the app:

- ➢ Start with the basics: Before diving into creating content, show them how to browse through the app, search for users or hashtags that interest them, and how to "like" or comment on videos they enjoy.

- ➢ Walk them through creating an account: While it may seem simple enough for us millennials and Gen Zers, creating an account on a new app can be intimidating for those who aren't as familiar with technology. Be patient and walk them through each step of setting up their profile.

➢ Show them different types of content: One of the best things about TikTok is that there is something for everyone - from cooking tutorials to dance challenges to funny skits. Show your family members examples of different types of content so they can get a sense of what they might want to create themselves.

➢ Help them find their niche: Once they've had some time browsing through the app, encourage them to start creating their own content. If they're not sure what to make videos about, help them find their niche based on their interests or hobbies.

Now that your loved ones are on TikTok and creating content, the fun really begins! Here are some ideas for how to keep in touch with family and friends through video content:

➢ Share updates on your life: No matter how far away you may be from each other, posting regular updates on your life can help you feel more connected. Whether it's a quick video of your morning routine or a longer vlog-style video of a recent trip you took, sharing pieces of your life can bring everyone closer together.

➢ Collaborate on videos: One fun way to mix things up is to collaborate with family members or friends on videos. This could mean doing a dance challenge together, creating a funny skit, or even just sharing a duet of a popular song. Not only is this a great way to have fun together, but it also gives your followers something different to watch.

➢ Celebrate milestones: Whether it's a birthday, graduation, or marriage anniversary - celebrating milestones through video content can be a great way to show your love and support from afar. Create special videos that highlight the person, or couple being celebrated and share them with everyone else in the family.

➢ Record special moments: From baby's first steps to important speeches at weddings - recording these special moments and sharing them with loved ones who couldn't be there can be incredibly meaningful. Plus, being able to relive those memories through video is priceless.

In conclusion, while TikTok may seem like an app only meant for young people, there are actually many benefits to having family members and friends join in on the fun. By teaching them the basics and encouraging them to create their own content, you can stay connected in new and exciting ways.

CHAPTER 19 - STAYING UP TO DATE WITH APP UPDATES

In this chapter, we'll be discussing the importance of staying up to date with app updates. As with any social media platform, TikTok regularly releases new features and updates that can impact your user experience as well as your audience engagement.

One way to stay informed about new trends or features within the app is by following official TikTok accounts on social media. The TikTok official Twitter feed or Facebook page are good places to start. Additionally, you can check the 'Discover' tab within the TikTok app, where you can browse popular hashtags and posts related to trending topics.

When a new feature is released on TikTok, it's important to take advantage of it and incorporate it into your content strategy. For example, when the 'Duet' feature was first introduced, many users were quick to use it in creative ways by collaborating with other users or reacting to popular videos. By utilizing new features in innovative ways, you can increase your chances of going viral and engaging with a wider audience.

New updates also impact post-performance metrics such as views and likes. For instance, if the algorithm changes how content is ranked on 'For You' pages or how often videos are recommended to users, this could significantly affect your post-performance.

Keeping track of these changes will help you adjust your posting strategy accordingly.

Another way to stay up to date with app updates is through influencer marketing campaigns. Influencers are typically given early access to new features and asked to share their thoughts and opinions via sponsored posts. Following influencers who specialize in topics relevant to your niche can help you spot emerging trends early on and learn how other creators are making the most out of new features.

In addition to staying informed about updates, it's important also keep an eye out for potential changes in privacy policies or community guidelines that might affect how you use the app. These types of announcements are usually made through official communications channels like email or within the app itself.

It's worth noting that not all updates will be relevant to you or your audience. For example, if a new feature is primarily aimed at younger users, it might not be suitable for your content. However, staying informed about these updates can still be useful because it can help you better understand the platform and its capabilities.

In conclusion, staying up to date with TikTok updates is crucial for maintaining an engaging presence on the app. By following official accounts on social media, keeping track of influencer marketing campaigns and being aware of changes in privacy policies or community guidelines, you'll be able to take advantage of new features as they are released and adapt your content strategy accordingly. Remember that not all updates will be relevant to your niche, but by learning about them you can keep informed about the latest trends and potential opportunities for growth.

CHAPTER 20 - LOOKING AHEAD & EMBRACING CHANGE

As we approach the end of this book, it's important to take a moment to look ahead and consider what the future may hold for TikTok as a social media platform. While no one can predict the future with complete accuracy, there are certainly some trends and changes that we can expect to see in the months and years to come.

One of the most exciting things about TikTok is its potential for growth. With over a billion active users already on the platform, it's clear that TikTok has struck a chord with people of all ages and backgrounds. However, there is still plenty of room for growth, particularly when it comes to user demographics.

While TikTok was originally thought of as an app for teenagers and young adults, we've already seen some significant shifts in this regard. In recent months, more and more older users have been joining the platform, drawn in by its unique blend of humour, creativity, and entertainment value. As these older users continue to discover TikTok and become more active on the platform, we can expect to see some changes in the types of content being created.

For example, we may begin to see more content aimed at an older audience - perhaps tutorials on gardening or home repair projects or funny skits about life as a grandparent. This expanding user demographic also opens up opportunities for brands who want to target an older demographic; they can now do so via influencer campaigns targeted towards specific age groups.

Of course, one thing that's certain about social media is that it's always changing. What's popular today may not be popular tomorrow - or even next week. This means that staying relevant on platforms like TikTok requires constant adaptation and evolution.

Take trends, for example. One day it might be dance challenges; another day everyone is trying their hand at comedy skits or lip-syncing popular songs. For influencers and businesses alike, keeping up with these trends is essential if they want to continue reaching new audiences and engaging with their existing followers.

But while it's important to stay on top of trends, it's equally important to be able to recognize when a trend has run its course. Continuing to beat a dead horse can lead to decreased engagement and even push away some followers who no longer find the content interesting.

So how can you prepare yourself for the changes that are sure to come in the world of TikTok?

First and foremost, it's essential to embrace change. Rather than fighting against new trends or trying to hold onto old ways of doing things, accept that social media is always evolving and be willing to try new things. This doesn't mean jumping on every bandwagon or trend that comes along; rather, it means being open-minded and willing to experiment with different types of content or approaches.

Another important factor in staying relevant on TikTok is being authentic. As more user's flood into the platform, competition for attention will only increase. In order to stand out from the crowd, influencers and businesses will need to offer something unique - whether that's humour, creativity, or valuable insights - while still staying true to themselves.

Finally, don't limit yourself in terms of what you think is possible on TikTok. While the platform is most commonly associated with entertainment content like funny skits or dance challenges, there are endless possibilities when it comes to what you can create and share on this app.

For example, we've already seen journalists using TikTok as a way of conveying news stories in a fun and accessible way; educators sharing bite-sized educational tutorials; non-profit organizations using the platform as a way of raising awareness about important issues; fitness experts creating quick workout routines...the list goes on.

As long as you're creative and willing to think outside the box, there's no telling what kind of amazing content you might be able to produce on this app.

In conclusion, TikTok has proven itself to be a dynamic and exciting platform with endless potential for growth and creativity. By staying open-minded, authentic, and always willing to experiment, influencers and businesses can continue to thrive on this app for years to come. So embrace change, stay true to yourself, and don't be afraid to push the boundaries of what's possible on TikTok - you never know what amazing opportunities may arise as a result.

And there we go, folks! This is the end of TikTok for Boomers. I hope you have thoroughly enjoyed reading this book and have gotten some valuable insights into how TikTok works and how it can be used by people from all age groups, including boomers.

As we come to the close of this book, I want to leave you with one final thought. Social media has transformed the way we communicate with each other and TikTok is no exception. It's a platform that allows people to share their creativity and express themselves through short videos.

While TikTok may seem overwhelming at first, it can provide an opportunity for boomers to connect with younger generations and stay engaged with the latest trends. We should embrace new technologies rather than shy away from them.

So, don't let the young people have all the fun on TikTok! Give it a try, experiment, play around – who knows what kind of content you might create? Thank you for taking the time to read my book and I hope it has inspired you to join this exciting social media movement.

ABOUT THE AUTHOR

Steve Quinn

Steve is a prolific author of many books on marketing, branding, business management and social media etc. He brings over 25 years experience to the table, creating many online shops and businesses along the way. Despite his busy schedule, he finds time to enjoy the simple pleasures in life. He is an avid gardener, and enjoys spending time at home on his small farm.